ELEPHANTS

A Photo Book of Wildlife Facts for Curious Kids

The Natural World Library

BRIGHT HABITAT
PRESS

Elephants

A Photo Book of Wildlife Facts for Curious Kids

Printed in the United States of America
ISBN-13: 979-8-88700-627-7 | Paperback

About This Book

Elephants introduces young readers to one of the world's most fascinating land animals through real photographs and simple, easy-to-understand facts.

This book is designed for curious kids ages 4–8 and presents one clear fact per page. Children will learn about elephant bodies, how elephants use their trunks, what they eat, how they live in family groups, and why elephants are important to the environments they live in.

With engaging images and age-appropriate information, this book supports early learning, observation skills, and a growing interest in animals and nature.

Elephants are the largest land animals on Earth.

Elephants are mammals, which means they are warm-blooded and have hair.

Elephants have long trunks that help them smell, breathe, and grab things.

An elephant's trunk has thousands of muscles and is very strong.

Elephants use their trunks to drink water and spray themselves to stay cool.

Elephants have large ears that help them cool their bodies.

Elephants can walk long distances to find food and water.

Elephants are strong and can push over trees with their bodies.

Elephants live in different habitats, including grasslands, forests, and savannas.

Elephants are herbivores, which means they eat plants.

Elephants eat grass, leaves, bark, and fruit.

An elephant can eat hundreds of pounds of food in one day.

Elephants live in family groups called herds.

Elephant herds are usually led by the oldest female, called the matriarch.

Elephants care for one another and help protect their family members.

Baby elephants are called calves.

Elephant calves stay close to their mothers for protection.

Elephants take care of their babies for many years.

Elephants use sounds and body movements to communicate.

Elephants can recognize other elephants and remember places they have visited.

Elephants live in Africa and Asia.

Asian

African

There are different species of elephants, including African and Asian elephants

Elephants play an important role in keeping ecosystems healthy.

Elephants help shape their environment by clearing paths and spreading seeds.

Bright Habitat Press creates educational picture books that help children explore animals, nature, and the world around them through real photographs and clear facts.

Our books are designed to support early learning and curiosity in young readers.

www.ingramcontent.com/pod-product-compliance
Lightning Source LLC
Chambersburg PA
CBHW060855270326
41934CB00002B/146